PIANO • VOCAL • GUITAR

50 TOP CLASSICS OF ROCK ERA

ISBN 0-634-01597-4

HAL•LEONARD®
CORPORATION

7777 W. BLUEMOUND RD. P.O. BOX 13819 MILWAUKEE, WI 53213

Visit Hal Leonard Online at
www.halleonard.com

50 TOP CLASSICS OF THE ROCK ERA

CONTENTS

AIN'T TOO PROUD TO BEG

Words and Music by EDWARD HOLLAND
and NORMAN WHITFIELD

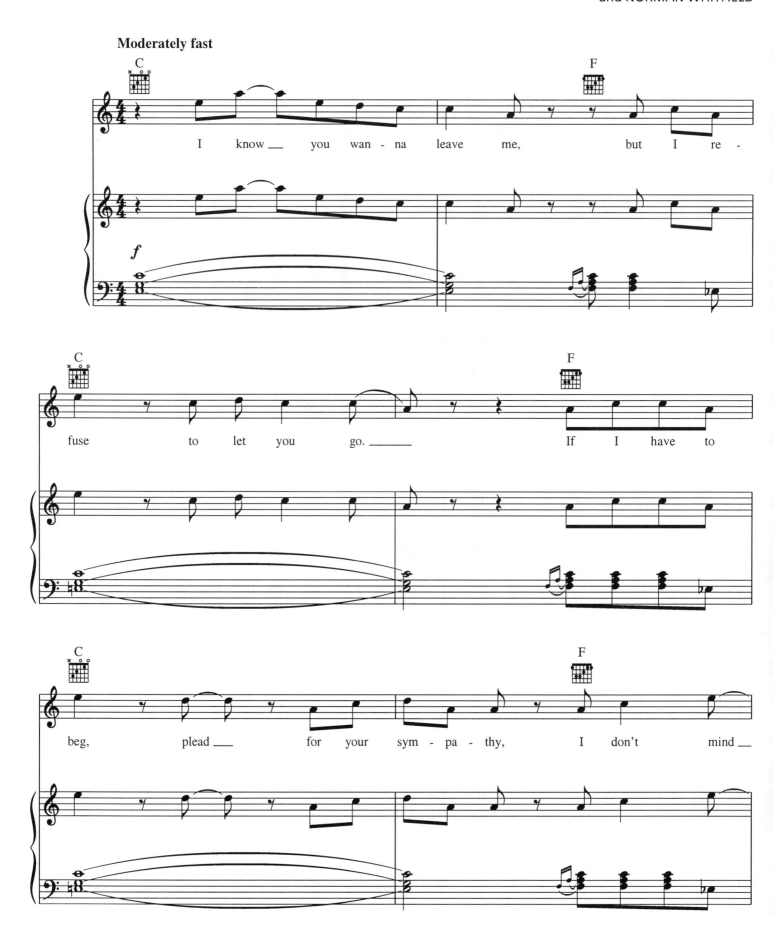

me, girl. ___ (Don't you go.) ___ If I have to

sleep on your door-step all ___ night and day ___ just to

keep you from walk-in' a-way, ___ let your

friends laugh; ___ e-ven this I can stand 'cause I

me, girl. ___ (Don't you go.) ___

Saxophone solo ad lib.

Play 3 times

Solo ends

Now I've got a

love so deep ___ in the pit of ___ my heart, and each

ALL SHOOK UP

Words and Music by OTIS BLACKWELL
and ELVIS PRESLEY

BOHEMIAN RHAPSODY

Words and Music by
FREDDIE MERCURY

Slowly

Is this the real life? Is this just fan-ta-sy? Caught in a land-slide, No es-

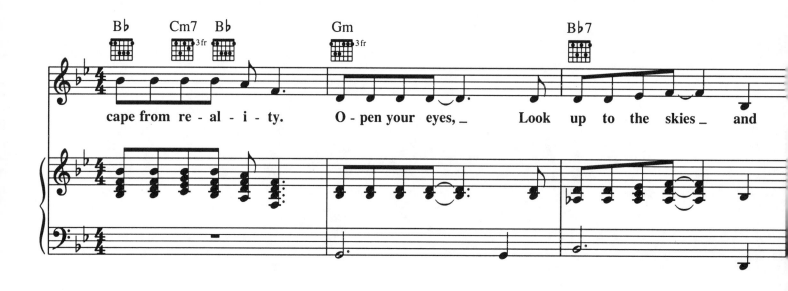

cape from re-al-i-ty. O-pen your eyes, _ Look up to the skies _ and

see, I'm just a poor boy, I need no sym-pa-thy, Be-cause I'm

CRYING

Words and Music by ROY ORBISON
and JOE MELSON

DON'T LET THE SUN GO DOWN ON ME

Words and Music by ELTON JOHN
and BERNIE TAUPIN

A DAY IN THE LIFE

Words and Music by JOHN LENNON
and PAUL McCARTNEY

DREAM ON

Words and Music by
STEVEN TYLER

EVERY BREATH YOU TAKE

Written and Composed by
STING

long for your _ em-brace. I keep cry - ing, ba - by, ba - by, please_

FIRE AND RAIN

Words and Music by
JAMES TAYLOR

Slowly

Verses 1&2:

Just yes-ter-day morn-ing they let me know__ you were gone__
Look down up-on me, Je-sus, you've got to help me make a stand__

Su-san the plans they made put an end to you
You've just got to see me through an-oth-er day

Verse 3:

GREAT BALLS OF FIRE

Words and Music by OTIS BLACKWELL
and JACK HAMMER

You shake my nerves and you rat-tle my brain. _ Too much love drives a man in-sane. _ You broke my will, but what a thrill. Good-ness gra-cious, great _ balls of fire! I laughed at love 'cause I thought it was fun-ny. You came a-long and you moved _

A HARD DAY'S NIGHT

Words and Music by JOHN LENNON
and PAUL McCARTNEY

HEARTACHE TONIGHT

Words and Music by JOHN DAVID SOUTHER, DON HENLEY,
GLENN FREY and BOB SEGER

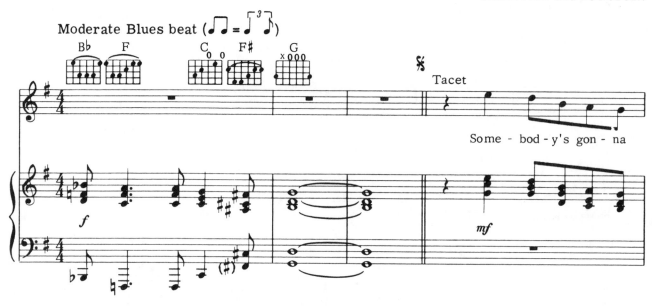

know. ___ There'll be a heart - ache to-night, ___ a heart-ache to-night, I know. ___

HEARTBREAK HOTEL

Words and Music by MAE BOREN AXTON,
TOMMY DURDEN and ELVIS PRESLEY

HEY JUDE

Words and Music by JOHN LENNON
and PAUL McCARTNEY

HOUND DOG

Words and Music by JERRY LEIBER
and MIKE STOLLER

I GOT YOU
(I Feel Good)

Words and Music by
JAMES BROWN

Moderately

Woh! I feel good. _____

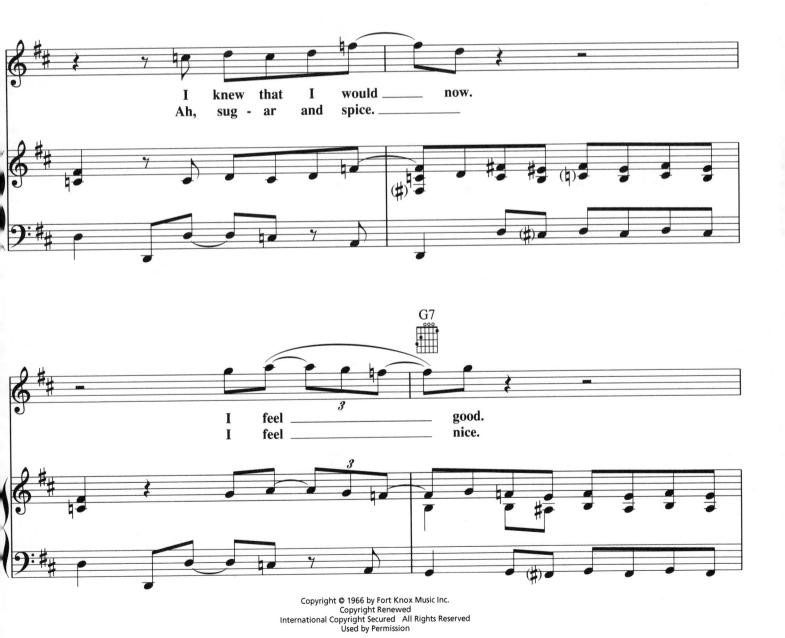

I knew that I would _____ now.
Ah, sug-ar and spice. _____

I feel _____ good.
I feel _____ nice.

I HEARD IT
THROUGH THE GRAPEVINE

Words and Music by NORMAN J. WHITFIELD
and BARRETT STRONG

D.S. al Coda

Peo - ple say be - lieve half _

CODA,

_ yeah, yeah, _ yeah. I heard it through the grape-vine, not much

Repeat and Fade

lon - ger would you be mine, ba - by. Yeah, _

IMAGINE

Words and Music by
JOHN LENNON

JAILHOUSE ROCK

featured in the Motion Picture THE BLUES BROTHERS
from SMOKEY JOE'S CAFE

Words and Music by JERRY LEIBER
and MIKE STOLLER

1. The war - den threw a par - ty in the
2.-5. *(See additional lyrics)*

coun - ty jail. ___ The pris - on band was there and they be -

gan to wail. The band was jump - in' and the joint be -

Additional Lyrics

2. Spider Murphy played the tenor saxophone
   Little Joe was blowin' on the slide trombone.
   The drummer boy from Illinois went crash, boon, bang;
   The whole rhythm section was the Purple Gang.
   (Chorus)

3. Number Forty-seven said to number Three:
   "You're the cutest jailbird I ever did see.
   I sure would be delighted with your company,
   Come on and do the Jailhouse Rock with me."
   (Chorus)

4. The sad sack was a-sittin' on a block of stone,
   Way over in the corner weeping all alone.
   The warden said: "Hey, Buddy, don't you be no square,
   If you can't find a partner, use a wooden chair!"
   (Chorus)

5. Shifty Henry said to Bugs: "For heaven's sake,
   No one's lookin', now's our chance to make a break."
   Bugsy turned to Shifty and he said: "Nix, nix;
   I wanna stick around a while and get my kicks."
   (Chorus)

LAYLA

Words and Music by ERIC CLAPTON
and JIM GORDON

Medium fast Rock

What will you do___ when you get lone - ly
I tried___ to give___ you con - so - la - tion
So make___ the best___ of the sit - u - a - tion

Original key: Eb minor. This edition has been transposed up one whole-step to be more playable.

LET IT BE

Words and Music by JOHN LENNON
and PAUL McCARTNEY

When I find my-self __ in times of trou-ble,
Instrumental

Moth-er Mar - y comes to me speak-ing words of wis - dom; let it

be. __ And in my hour of dark - ness, she is

MAGGIE MAY

Words and Music by ROD STEWART
and MARTIN QUITTENTON

2. You lured me away from home, just to save you from being alone.
You stole my soul, that's a pain I can do without.
All I needed was a friend to lend a guiding hand.
But you turned into a lover, and, Mother, what a lover! You wore me out.
All you did was wreck my bed, and in the morning kick me in the head.
Oh, Maggie, I couldn't have tried any more.

3. You lured me away from home, 'cause you didn't want to be alone.
You stole my heart, I couldn't leave you if I tried.
I suppose I could collect my books and get back to school.
Or steal my Daddy's cue and make a living out of playing pool,
Or find myself a rock and roll band that needs a helpin' hand.
Oh, Maggie, I wish I'd never seen your face. **(To Coda)**

LITTLE DEUCE COUPE

Music by BRIAN WILSON
Words by ROGER CHRISTIAN

don't e - ven try.__ And if it had a set of wings, man, I know I could fly,__ she's my
stroked and she's bored.. She'll do a hun-dred and for-ty with the top end floored, she's my

lit - tle deuce coupe you don't know__ what I got.__
lit - tle deuce coupe you don't know__ what I got.__

Just a

She's got a com-pe - ti - tion clutch, with

ME AND BOBBY MCGEE

Words and Music by KRIS KRISTOFFERSON
and FRED FOSTER

Vocal written one octave higher than sung.

Lord.

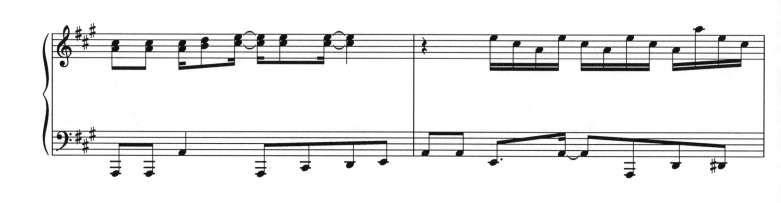

MY GIRL

Words and Music by WILLIAM "SMOKEY" ROBINSON
and RONALD WHITE

(Hey, hey, hey.)

(Hey, hey, hey.)

Ooh, _____ hoo, _____ yeah. ___

OH, PRETTY WOMAN

Words and Music by ROY ORBISON
and BILL DEES

OPERATOR
(That's Not the Way It Feels)

Words and Music by
JIM CROCE

I've learned to take it well. __ I on-ly wish my words __ could just con-vince my-self __

__ that it just was-n't real, _____ but that's not the way it feels.

OUR HOUSE

Words and Music by
GRAHAM NASH

PAPA WAS A ROLLIN' STONE

Words and Music by NORMAN WHITFIELD
and BARRETT STRONG

PENNY LANE

Words and Music by JOHN LENNON
and PAUL McCARTNEY

PIANO MAN

Words and Music by
BILLY JOEL

ROCK AROUND THE CLOCK

Words and Music by MAX C. FREEDMAN
and JIMMY DeKNIGHT

ROXANNE

Written and Composed by
STING

SHE'S ALWAYS A WOMAN

Words and Music by
BILLY JOEL

D. S. al Coda

Coda

most she will do is throw sha-dows at you But she's al-ways a wom-an to

me. (Hum) (Hum)

rit.

rit.

STAND BY ME

Words and Music by BEN E. KING,
JERRY LEIBER and MIKE STOLLER

START ME UP

Words and Music by MICK JAGGER
and KEITH RICHARDS

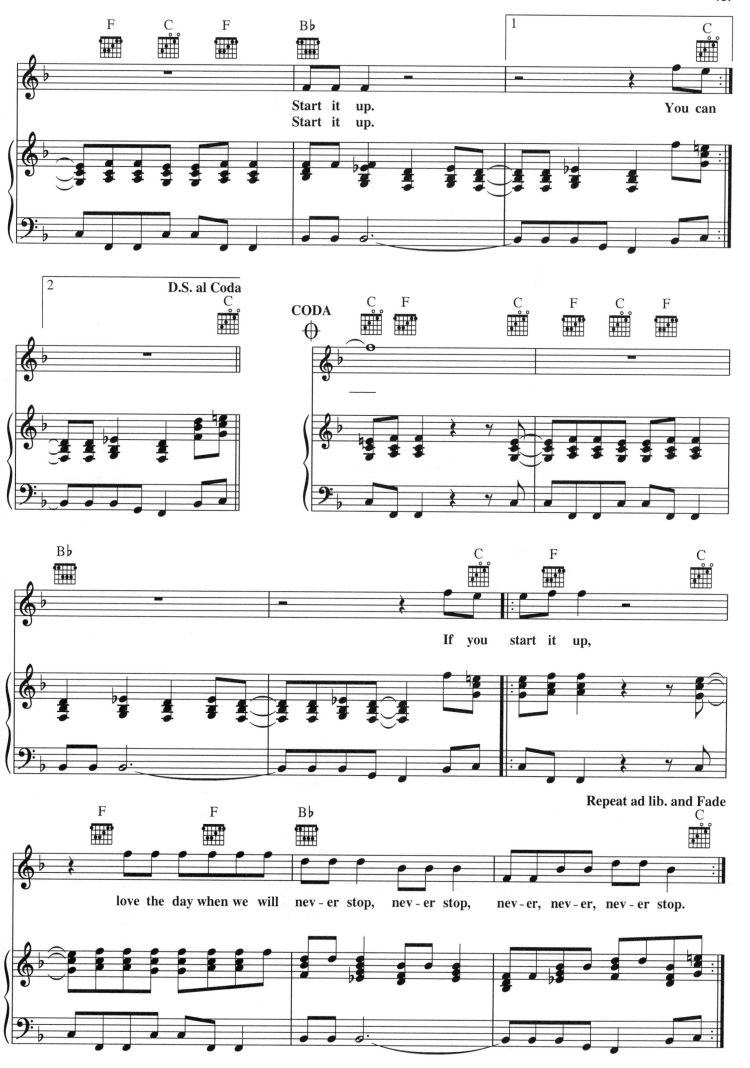

STAYIN' ALIVE

Words and Music by BARRY GIBB,
MAURICE GIBB and ROBIN GIBB

Some-bod-y help me. _____ Some-bod-y help_ me, yeah._

Fm7

Bb7

_____ Life go-in' no-where. _____

Fm7

Some-bod-y help_ me, yeah._____ I'm stay-in' a-live._

Repeat and Fade

STRAWBERRY FIELDS FOREVER

Words and Music by JOHN LENNON
and PAUL McCARTNEY

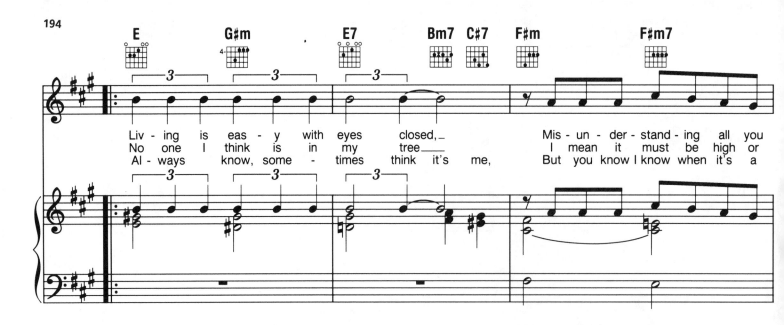

E   G#m   E7   Bm7   C#7   F#m   F#m7

Liv - ing is eas - y with eyes closed,   Mis - un - der - stand - ing all you
No one I think is in my tree   I mean it must be high or
Al - ways know, some - times think it's me, But you know I know when it's a

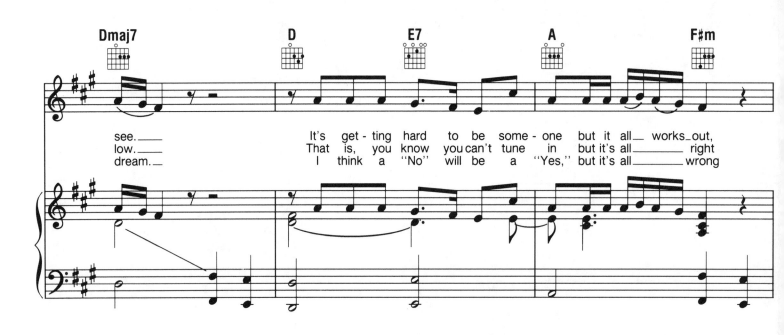

Dmaj7   D   E7   A   F#m

see.   It's get - ting hard to be some - one but it all works out,
low.   That is, you know you can't tune in but it's all right
dream.   I think a "No" will be a "Yes," but it's all wrong

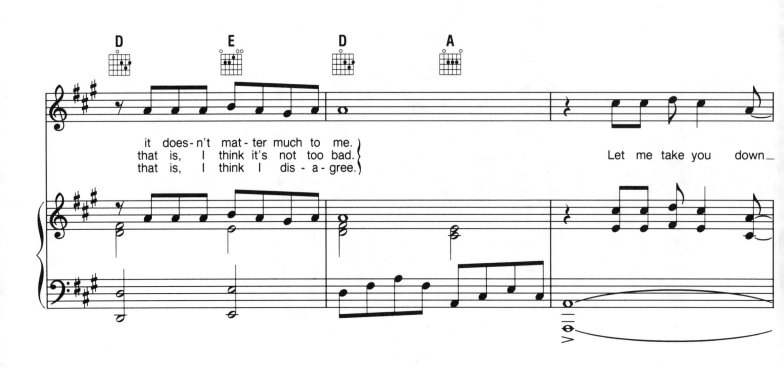

D   E   D   A

it doesn't mat - ter much to me.)
that is, I think it's not too bad. }
that is, I think I dis - a - gree.)

Let me take you down

SUNSHINE OF YOUR LOVE

Words and Music by JACK BRUCE,
PETE BROWN and ERIC CLAPTON

SURFIN' U.S.A.

Words and Music by
CHUCK BERRY

SUPERSTITION

Words and Music by
STEVIE WONDER

Moderate Funk

Ver-y su-per-sti-

- tious, _   writ-ings on the wall. _
- tious. _   Wash your face and hands. _
- tious. _   Noth-ing more to say. _

Ver-y su-per-sti - tious, _   lad-der's 'bout _ to fall. _
Rid me of the prob - lems. _   Do all that _ you can. _
Ver-y su-per-sti - tious. _   The dev-il's on _ his way. _

TEACH YOUR CHILDREN

Words and Music by
GRAHAM NASH

You who are on the road ___

To Coda ⊕

and know they

love _____ you.

(Can you
And you

WALK THIS WAY

Words and Music by STEVEN TYLER
and JOE PERRY

Back - stroke lov - er al - ways hid - in' 'neath the cov - ers till I
See - saw swing - er with the boys in the school and your
School girl sweet - ies with a class - y, kind - a sass - y lit - tle
See - saw swing - er with the boys in the school and your

talked to your dad - dy, he say, _____ he said, "You
feet fly - in' up in the air, _____ sing - in',
skirts climb - in' way up their knees; _____ there was
feet fly - in' up in the air, _____ sing - in',

best things of lov - in' with her sis - ter and her cous - in on - ly
me she was fool - in', 'cause she knew what she was do - in' when I
next door neigh-bor with a daugh-ter had a fa - vor, so I
me she was fool - in', 'cause she knew what she was do - in' when she

1,3

A

start - ed with a lit - tle kiss _____ like this.
knowed love was here to stay ___
gave her just a lit - tle kiss _____ like this.
told me how to walk this way. ___

no chord

THAT'LL BE THE DAY

Words and Music by JERRY ALLISON,
NORMAN PETTY and BUDDY HOLLY

TIME IN A BOTTLE

Words and Music by
JIM CROCE

TWIST AND SHOUT

Words and Music by BERT RUSSELL
and PHIL MEDLEY

mine. *(Like I knew you would)*
(Let me know you're mine)

Well, shake it up ba-

Ah   Ah

WE ARE THE CHAMPIONS

Words and Music by
FREDDIE MERCURY

WHAT'S GOING ON

Words and Music by MARVIN GAYE,
AL CLEVELAND and RENALDO BENSON

WILD THING

Words and Music by
CHIP TAYLOR

WILD THING,   You make my heart sing.

You make eve - ry - thing ___ groov - y. ___

Repeat and Fade

WILD   THING.

YOU REALLY GOT ME

Words and Music by
RAY DAVIES

1. Girl you real-ly got me go-ing you got me
2. See don't ev-er set me free___ I al-ways
3. See don't ev-er set me free___ I al-ways

so I don't know what I'm do-ing___
wan-na be by your side _____
wan-na be by your side _____

Yeah
Girl } you real-ly got me now You got me
Girl

Contemporary Classics

Your favorite songs for piano, voice and guitar.

The Definitive Rock 'n' Roll Collection

A classic collection of the best songs from the early rock 'n' roll years – 1955-1966. 97 songs, including: Barbara Ann • Chantilly Lace • Dream Lover • Duke of Earl • Earth Angel • Great Balls of Fire • Louie, Louie • Rock Around the Clock • Ruby Baby • Runaway • (Seven Little Girls) Sitting in the Back Seat • Stay • Surfin' U.S.A. • Wild Thing • Woolly Bully • and more.

00490195 ....$27.95

The Big Book of Rock

78 of rock's biggest hits, including: Addicted to Love • American Pie • Born to Be Wild • Cold As Ice • Dust in the Wind • Free Bird • Goodbye Yellow Brick Road • Groovin' • Hey Jude • I Love Rock 'N' Roll • Lay Down Sally • Layla • Livin' on a Prayer • Louie Louie • Maggie May • Me and Bobby McGee • Monday, Monday • Owner of a Lonely Heart • Shout • Walk This Way • We Didn't Start the Fire • You Really Got Me • and more.

00311566 ....$19.95

Big Book of Movie Music

Features 73 classic songs from 72 movies: Beauty and the Beast • Change the World • Eye of the Tiger • I Finally Found Someone • The John Dunbar Theme • Somewhere in Time • Stayin' Alive • Take My Breath Away • Unchained Melody • The Way You Look Tonight • You've Got a Friend in Me • Zorro's Theme • more.

00311582 ....$19.95

The Best Rock Songs Ever

70 of the best rock songs from yesterday and today, including: All Day and All of the Night • All Shook Up • Ballroom Blitz • Bennie and the Jets • Blue Suede Shoes • Born to Be Wild • Boys Are Back in Town • Every Breath You Take • Faith • Free Bird • Hey Jude • I Still Haven't Found What I'm Looking For • Livin' on a Prayer • Lola • Louie Louie • Maggie May • Money • (She's) Some Kind of Wonderful • Takin' Care of Business • Walk This Way • We Didn't Start the Fire • We Got the Beat • Wild Thing • more!

00490424 ....$17.95

#1 Songs of the '90s

21 top hits as listed on the *Billboard* Hot 100 Singles Chart. Songs include: All My Life • Candle in the Wind 1997 • The Power of Love • The Sign • and more.

00310018 ....$12.95

Motown Anthology

This songbook commemorates Motown's 40th Anniversary with 68 songs, background information on this famous record label, and lots of photos. Songs include: ABC • Baby Love • Ben • Dancing in the Street • Easy • For Once in My Life • My Girl • Shop Around • The Tracks of My Tears • War • What's Going On • You Can't Hurry Love • and many more.

00310367 ....$19.95

"My Heart Will Go On (Love Theme from 'Titanic')" & 23 More Songs from Today's Hit Movies

Includes these megahits: (I Love You) For Sentimental Reasons (*As Good As It Gets*) • You Must Love Me (*Evita*) • Miss Misery (*Good Will Hunting*) • You Sexy Thing (*The Full Monty*) • I Say a Little Prayer (*My Best Friend's Wedding*) • and more.

00310417 ....$10.95

Women of Modern Rock

25 songs from contemporary chanteuses, including: As I Lay Me Down • Connection • Feed the Tree • Galileo • Here and Now • Look What Love Has Done • Love Sneakin' Up on You • Walking on Broken Glass • You Oughta Know • Zombie • and more.

00310093 ....$14.95

Jock Rock Hits

32 stadium-shaking favorites, including: Another One Bites the Dust • The Boys Are Back in Town • Freeze-Frame • Gonna Make You Sweat (Everybody Dance Now) • I Got You (I Feel Good) • Na Na Hey Hey Kiss Him Goodbye • Rock & Roll – Part II (The Hey Song) • Shout • Tequila • We Are the Champions • We Will Rock You • Whoomp! (There It Is) • Wild Thing • and more.

00310105 ....$14.95

Rock Ballads

31 sentimental favorites, including: All for Love • Bed of Roses • Dust in the Wind • Everybody Hurts • Right Here Waiting • Tears in Heaven • and more.

00311673 ....$14.95

Classic Collections Of Your Favorite Songs

arranged for piano, voice, and guitar.

Beautiful Ballads

A massive collection of 87 songs, including: April In Paris • Autumn In New York • Call Me Irresponsible • Cry Me A River • I Wish You Love • I'll Be Seeing You • If • Imagine • Isn't It Romantic? • It's Impossible (Somos Novios) • Mona Lisa • Moon River • People • The Way We Were • A Whole New World (Aladdin's Theme) • and more.
00311679 ....$17.95

Irving Berlin Anthology

A comprehensive collection of 61 timeless songs with a bio, song background notes, and photos. Songs include: Always • Blue Skies • Cheek To Cheek • God Bless America • Marie • Puttin' On The Ritz • Steppin' Out With My Baby • There's No Business Like Show Business • White Christmas • (I Wonder Why?) You're Just In Love • and more.
00312493 ....$19.95

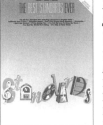

The Best Standards Ever Volume 1 (A-L)

72 beautiful ballads, including: All The Things You Are • Bewitched • Can't Help Lovin' Dat Man • Don't Get Around Much Anymore • Getting To Know You • God Bless' The Child • Hello, Young Lovers • I Got It Bad And That Ain't Good • It's Only A Paper Moon • I've Got You Under My Skin • The Lady Is A Tramp • Little White Lies.
00359231 ....$15.95

The Best Standards Ever Volume 2 (M-Z)

72 songs, including: Makin' Whoopee • Misty • Moonlight In Vermont • My Funny Valentine • Old Devil Moon • The Party's Over • People Will Say We're In Love • Smoke Gets In Your Eyes • Strangers In The Night • Tuxedo Junction • Yesterday.
00359232 ....$15.95

The Big Book of Standards

86 classics essential to any music library, including: April In Paris • Autumn In New York • Blue Skies • Cheek To Cheek • Heart And Soul • I Left My Heart In San Francisco • In The Mood • Isn't It Romantic? • Mona Lisa • Moon River • The Nearness Of You • Out Of Nowhere • Spanish Eyes • Star Dust • Stella By Starlight • That Old Black Magic • They Say It's Wonderful • What Now My Love • and more.
00311667 ....$19.95

Classic Jazz Standards

56 jazz essentials: All the Things You Are • Don't Get Around Much Anymore • How Deep Is the Ocean • In the Wee Small Hours of the Morning • Polka Dots and Moonbeams • Satin Doll • Skylark • Tangerine • Tenderly • What's New? • and more.
00310310 ....$16.95

I'll Be Seeing You: 50 Songs of World War II

A salute to the music and memories of WWII, including a year-by-year chronology of events on the homefront, dozens of photos, and 50 radio favorites of the GIs and their families back home, including: Boogie Woogie Bugle Boy • Don't Sit Under The Apple Tree (With Anyone Else But Me) • I Don't Want To Walk Without You • I'll Be Seeing You • Moonlight In Vermont • There's A Star-Spangled Banner Waving Somewhere • You'd Be So Nice To Come Home To • and more.
00311698 ....$19.95

Best of Cole Porter

38 of his classics, including: All Of You • Anything Goes • Be A Clown • Don't Fence Me In • I Get A Kick Out Of You • In The Still Of The Night • Let's Do It (Let's Fall In Love) • Night And Day • You Do Something To Me • and many
00311577 ....$14.95

Big Band Favorites

A great collection of 70 of the best Swing Era songs, including: East of the Sun • Honeysuckle Rose • I Can't Get Started with You • I'll Be Seeing You • In the Mood • Let's Get Away from It All • Moonglow • Moonlight in Vermont • Opus One • Stompin' at the Savoy • Tuxedo Junction • more!
00310445 ....$16.95

The Best of Rodgers & Hammerstein

A capsule of 26 classics from this legendary duo. Songs include: Climb Ev'ry Mountain • Edelweiss • Getting To Know You • I'm Gonna Wash That Man Right Outa My Hair • My Favorite Things • Oklahoma • The Surrey With The Fringe On Top • You'll Never Walk Alone • and more.
00308210 ....$12.95

The Best Songs Ever

80 must-own classics, including: All I Ask Of You • Body And Soul • Crazy • Endless Love • Fly Me To The Moon • Here's That Rainy Day • In The Mood • Love Me Tender • Memory • Moonlight In Vermont • My Funny Valentine • People • Satin Doll • Save The Best For Last • Somewhere Out There • Strangers In The Night • Tears In Heaven • A Time For Us • The Way We Were • When I Fall In Love • You Needed Me • and more.
00359224 .... $19.95

Torch Songs

Sing your heart out with this collection of 59 sultry jazz and big band melancholy masterpieces, including: Angel Eyes • Cry Me A River • I Can't Get Started • I Got It Bad And That Ain't Good • I'm Glad There Is You • Lover Man (Oh, Where Can You Be?) • Misty • My Funny Valentine • Stormy Weather • and many more! 224 pages.
00490446 ....$16.95

0899

THE ULTIMATE SERIES

This comprehensive series features jumbo collections of piano/vocal arrangements with guitar chords. Each volume features an outstanding selection of your favorite songs. Collect them all for the ultimate music library!

Broadway Gold

100 show tunes from a wide variety of Broadway's biggest hits: Beauty and the Beast • Bewitched • Brotherhood of Man • Do-Re-Mi • Guys and Dolls • Happy Talk • I Ain't Down Yet • I Love Paris • I Whistle a Happy Tune • It Only Takes a Moment • The Lady Is a Tramp • Let Me Entertain You • Mame • Memory • My Funny Valentine • Oklahoma • Old Devil Moon • The Rain in Spain • Soon It's Gonna Rain • Some Enchanted Evening • Seventy-Six Trombones • Standing on the Corner • Summer Nights • There Is Nothin' Like a Dame • Till There Was You • Tomorrow • What I Did for Love • With One Look • many more.
00361396 . . . .$21.95

Broadway Platinum

A collection of 100 popular Broadway show tunes, featuring the hits: As Long As He Needs Me • Bali Ha'i • Beauty and the Beast • Camelot • Consider Yourself • Everything's Coming Up Roses • Getting to Know You • Gigi • Do You Hear the People Sing • Hello, Young Lovers • I'll Be Seeing You • If Ever I Would Leave You • My Favorite Things • On a Clear Day • People • September Song • She Loves Me • Sun and Moon • Try to Remember • Younger Than Springtime • Who Can I Turn To • many more.
00311496 . . . .$19.95

Christmas – 100 Seasonal Favorites

Includes: Angels We Have Heard on High • Away in a Manger • Bring a Torch, Jeannette, Isabella • Carol of the Bells • Dance of the Sugar Plum Fairy • Deck the Hall • The First Noel • Frosty the Snow Man • Gesu Bambino • Good King Wenceslas • Happy Holiday • Hark! the Herald Angels Sing • Here We Come A-Wassailing • A Holly Jolly Christmas • I Heard the Bells on Christmas Day • It Came upon the Midnight Clear • Jesu, Joy of Man's Desiring • Jingle-Bell Rock • Jolly Old St. Nicholas • Joy to the World • Let It Snow! Let It Snow! Let It Snow! • March of the Toys • Nuttin' for Christmas • O Christmas Tree • O Come, All Ye Faithful (Adeste Fideles) • O Holy Night • Rudolph the Red-Nosed Reindeer • Silent Night • Silver Bells • Up on the Housetop • What Child Is This? • and more.
00361399 . . . .$19.95

Country

Over 90 of your favorite country hits in one collection! Features: A Rainy Night in Georgia • Boot Scootin' Boogie • Brand New Man • Chattahoochie • Could I Have This Dance • Crazy • Down at the Twist And Shout • Folsom Prison Blues • Hey, Good Lookin' • Lucille • Neon Moon • She Is His Only Need • Southern Nights • When She Cries • Where've You Been • and more.
00310036 . . . .$19.95

Gospel – 100 Songs of Devotion

Includes: El Shaddai • His Eye Is on the Sparrow • How Great Thou Art • Just a Closer Walk With Thee • Lead Me, Guide Me • (There'll Be) Peace in the Valley (For Me) • Precious Lord, Take My Hand • Wings of a Dove • more.
00241009 . . . .$19.95

Jazz Standards

Over 100 great jazz favorites, including: Ain't Misbehavin' • All of Me • Bernie's Tune • Come Rain or Come Shine • From This Moment On • Girl Talk • Here's That Rainy Day • I'll Take Romance • Imagination • Li'l Darlin' • Manhattan • Moonglow • Moonlight in Vermont • A Night in Tunisia • The Party's Over • Route 66 • Slightly Out of Tune • Solitude • Star Dust • You Turned the Tables on Me • and more.
00361407 . . . .$19.95

Love and Wedding Songbook

90 songs of devotion including: The Anniversary Waltz • Canon in D • Endless Love • For All We Know • Forever and Ever, Amen • Just the Way You Are • Longer • The Lord's Prayer • Love Me Tender • One Hand, One Heart • Somewhere • Sunrise, Sunset • Through the Years • Trumpet Voluntary • and many, many more!
00361445 . . . .$19.95

FOR MORE INFORMATION, SEE YOUR LOCAL MUSIC DEALER, OR WRITE TO:

HAL•LEONARD® CORPORATION
7777 W. BLUEMOUND RD. P.O. BOX 13819 MILWAUKEE, WI 53213

http://www.halleonard.com

Prices, contents, and availability subject to change without notice.
Availability and pricing may vary outside the U.S.A.

Movie Music

Over 70 favorites from the big screen, including: Also Sprach Zarathustra • Can You Feel the Love Tonight • Chariots of Fire • Cinema Paridiso • Cruella De Vil • Driving Miss Daisy • Easter Parade • Forrest Gump • Moon River • That Thing You Do! • Viva Las Vegas • The Way We Were • When I Fall in Love • and more.
00310240 . . . .$17.95

Rock 'N' Roll

100 classics, including: All Shook Up • Bye Bye Love • Chantilly Lace • Duke of Earl • Gloria • Hello Mary Lou • I Only Want to Be With You • It's My Party • Johnny B. Goode • The Loco-Motion • Lollipop • Rock Around the Clock • Surfin' U.S.A. • A Teenager in Love • The Twist • Wooly Bully • Yakety Yak • and more.
00361411 . . . .$21.95

Singalong!

100 of the best-loved popular songs ever: Ain't Misbehavin' • All of Me • Beer Barrel Polka • California, Here I Come • The Candy Man • Crying in the Chapel • Edelweiss • Feelings • Five Foot Two, Eyes of Blue • For Me and My Gal • Goodnight Irene • I Left My Heart in San Francisco • Indiana • It's a Small World • Que Sera, Sera • This Land Is Your Land • Too Fat Polka • When Irish Eyes Are Smiling • and more.
00361418 . . . .$17.95

Standard Ballads

100 mellow masterpieces, including: Angel Eyes • Body and Soul • Darn That Dream • Day By Day • Easy to Love • In The Still of the Night • Isn't It Romantic? • Misty • Mona Lisa • Moon River • My Funny Valentine • Smoke Gets in Your Eyes • When I Fall in Love • and more.
00310246 . . . .$19.95

Swing Standards

Over 90 songs to get you swinging, including: Bandstand Boogie • Boogie Woogie Bugle Boy • Cherokee • Don't Get Around Much Anymore • Heart and Soul • How High the Moon • In the Mood • Moonglow • Satin Doll • Sentimental Journey • Witchcraft • and more.
00310245 . . . .$19.95

0300